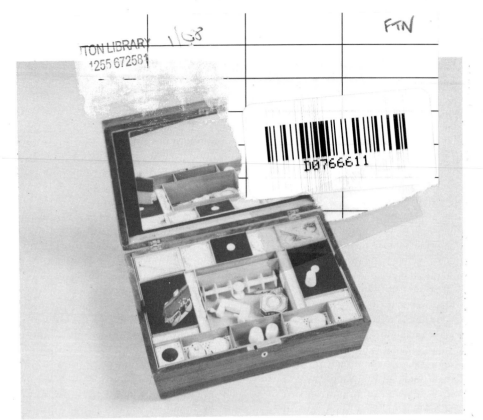

An early nineteenth-century workbox made of rosewood. The inside has been partially restored. It contains several matching ivory cotton barrels, an ivory tapemeasure, needlecase, emery, part of a clamp, a multiple reel, a single reel, an ivory thimble and a tatting shuttle. The charming cottage pincushion has been beautifully embroidered.

NEEDLEWORK TOOLS

A guide to collecting

Eleanor Johnson

Shire Publications Ltd

CONTENTS

Copyright © 1978 by Eleanor Johnson. First published 1978, reprinted 1980, 1982, 1983, 1985, 1986, 1987. Shire Album 38. ISBN 0 85263 446 3.

Printed in Great Britain by C. I. Thomas & Sons (Haverfordwest) Ltd.

A miniature sewing machine, about 9 inches high (225 mm), probably late Victorian. It was the introduction of the sewing machine in the 1870s which made it so much quicker and easier to make clothing and other articles and so led to the decline in the popularity of many of the attractive hand-made accessories and those less essential in the age of the machine.

An early nineteenth-century round sewing case, with a mirror in the lid, lined in blue silk, and with ribbon loops to hold tools. An oval mid nineteenth-century sewing case, complete with matching fittings in steel. Both cases are leather-covered.

INTRODUCTION

Needlework has a long history, as also have the more mundane tools associated with it: for example, pins, needles and scissors. In earlier times necessity was the mother of invention, and thorns were used for pins, fish bones and carved bone for needles, and primitive scissors were made of iron. Sewing was an essential part of daily life for the making of all clothes in skins and coarsely woven materials. Naturally, as time went on, improvements were made, both in the tools and in the fabrics used. Craftsmen were quick to use their skills in producing more efficient, attractive tools in more elaborate and expensive materials.

There are references to needlework tools from Roman times, but they increased greatly in the sixteenth, seventeenth and eighteenth centuries until, for our present purpose, the nineteenth century became the most prolific period in mention and manufacture.

Changing modes of life and social customs elevated needlework from a pure necessity to an art and social grace. Women of the middle and upper classes had ample leisure, as servants did most of the work of running the household for them. Needlework and many similar activities were popular diversions for occupying their time. During Regency and Victorian times, for ladies in society, needlework, knotting and tatting were important social accomplishments — tatting because a graceful movement is involved. Needlework required skill and provided scope for the exercise of good taste and ingenuity in the use of a wide variety of materials and patterns in the making of dainty and exquisitely conceived articles. Among these are miniature pincushions in patchwork and small purses. The custom of taking

3

needlework to large gatherings or private social occasions continued into the early part of the nineteenth century and while those who preferred played cards it was quite polite for others to sit and chat and occupy themselves with their embroidery or other work. For this purpose ladies carried small sewing cases or etuis, sometimes called the ladies' companion. These were in a variety of sizes and materials, with a varying number of implements inside. Some of the pretty articles they had made or been given as presents would be included, especially needlecases and pincushions, and these would be passed round for admiring comment and as topics for conversation.

Ladies also carried small items with them when out visiting or shopping, especially pin wheels, in order to effect immediate repairs should a garment become torn. These were often concealed in large pockets in their voluminous skirts or in little drawstring bags. They could also be worn on a chatelaine suspended from the waist by a large hook; the earliest ones were very decorative in cut and faceted steel, but these were later superseded by silver and silver plate. The chatelaine had a number of chains suspended from the central clip, with a different item hanging at the end of each. There might be a thimble in a bucket, scissors in a sheath, pincushion, needlecase, pencil, buttonhook, scent bottle, or notebook. In the earliest examples the chains terminate in a split ring, but later ones have a swivel clip to attach the necessary requisites. Chatelaines developed in medieval times, from the necessity for the lady of the house (after whom they are named) to carry the keys to her storage chests on her person. Precious tea and other commodities were kept safely in this way before the appearance of cupboards. They went out of fashion in the late nineteenth century but were revived by Queen Alexandra as a fashion accessory.

For the ladies so busily occupied with their various activities there were in the towns many shops which sold the accessories, or 'toys' as they were called, and the choice was wide. In the country pedlars or packmen visited homes offering the ladies of the household their various wares. In addition there were the popular annual fairs where goods were displayed in booths. Stourbridge Fair was one of the largest and most popular, not only with the local country people but also with ladies of fashion, who drove long distances in their carriages to visit them and stroll among the stalls inspecting the latest trifles.

In the days when the parlour was an important feature of the Victorian home, furnished with so many 'whatnots' and small tables, an outlet was readily to hand for all the delightful small articles made by the accomplished needlewomen. It was popular to give the dainty trifles they made as presents, which were then displayed for all to admire.

For use at home, many needlewomen owned a workbox elaborately decorated with brass, ivory or mother-of-pearl. Most commonly these are rectangular, with a loose lift-out tray divided into compartments and covering a space underneath for additional accessories or work in progress. During the early nineteenth century the tray was fitted with matching sets of cotton barrels, to hold cotton, together with pin boxes, thimble, tapemeasure, thread waxer and emery. Later boxes had cotton-ball holders topped with mother-of-pearl, with the other items to match, or wooden cotton reels in the appropriate compartments.

During the Victorian era, with the coming of the railways and improved roads, travel and visits further afield became easier and more popular. The growth of the tourist industry followed, and the manufacture of souvenirs was vastly increased. The variety of goods produced for this purpose is infinite, and among them are many of the needlework and related items so prized by the collector today and originally given as gifts by those who had visited the growing number of fashionable resorts.

There are several types of souvenir wares which the collector of needlework tools may find. *Tunbridge Ware* was made at Tunbridge Wells in Kent, and most of the pieces now turning up date-from the early nineteenth century on-

A collection of sewing sets. Left to right, top row: two ladies' companions, the first in tooled green leather, with scent bottle, thimble, needlecase, scissors, pencil, tweezers and tatting shuttle; the second, in finely decorated red leather, in the shape of a book. The top has 'Ladies' Companion' in gold lettering on the spine. It contains ivory notebook, needlecase, thimble and penknife. Second row: early nineteenth-century tiny leather-covered necessaire, containing scissors, file, bodkin and tweezers in steel; charming red leather box, lined in red silk, containing waxer and thimble (not the originals) and a pincushion, which is the original; etui, with a matching set of fine silver tools in a delicate design. Bottom: flower-decorated turquoise enamel sewing compendium. The top is a thimble which unscrews to reveal a metal cotton holder and folding scissors, together with a paper packet of needles.

Four pieces of Tunbridge Ware. The delightful kettle pincushion, round pincushion, and combined waxer and pincushion are all Stickware, with pincushions in blue velvet. The sliding-top pincushion box is decorated with Mosaic, and is covered in blue cotton.

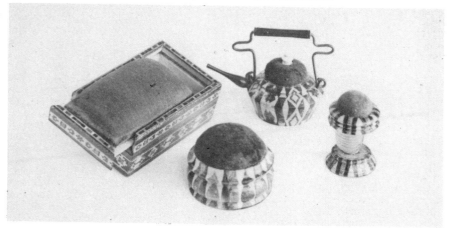

wards. The earliest were decorated with painted lines on light-coloured wood. It was followed by *Stickware*, articles turned from a group of pieces of different-coloured woods glued into a stick. Then there was *Mosaic* – fine slices cut from a similarly made stick and used to decorate wooden articles, much of the undecorated part being made of rosewood.

Scottish Transfer Ware or *Mauchline*, so called because it was first made in the Ayrshire village of Mauchline, is another common type. Most of the pieces now found are decorated with a black transfer print on a sycamore-wood base. They also date from the early nineteenth century and often feature pictures of resorts. A later type is similar, but a stuck-on photograph replaces the transfer print.

Tartan Ware also came from Scotland, in the first quarter of the nineteenth century, and is said to have greatly increased in popularity when Queen Victoria built Balmoral. Originally the tartan pattern was painted on the wooden articles, but later this was replaced by the use of tartan paper glued to the wooden base.

Fern Ware again consists of a wooden base, decorated in the earliest pieces with real ferns, but those most commonly found now have applied colour decoration. This ware dates from the early twentieth century.

A number of other small items in wood are painted black and decorated with coloured pictures and verses.

A less common souvenir ware, mainly pincushions and needlecases, though tapemeasures may be found, is decorated with a coloured print under glass, with a mirror on the reverse side of the article.

In addition to these souvenir wares many needlework accessories will be found made of gold, silver, silver gilt, silver plate, mother-of-pearl, tortoise-shell (with or without pique in gold or silver), ivory, vegetable ivory (the kernel of the corozo nut, usually darker coloured), wood, fabric, leather, horn, bone, jet, beadwork and straw-work (fine pieces of dyed, cut straw glued to a wooden base).

Collection of items in Mauchline or Scottish Transfer Ware. Left to right: a cotton-reel box (see the holes in the side for the thread to emerge). It has a label advertising J. & P. Coats sewing cotton inside the lid. The transfer print on the outside of the lid is of Grange in Borrowdale. A bottle shaped thimble holder. A milk churn-shaped tapemeasure, with a print of Ambleside. A saucepan thimble holder (the lid removed), and a slim round pincushion with a print of Margate.

Five pieces of Tartan Ware in Royal Stewart Tartan. Left to right: a slim trefoil-shaped pincushion; a tatting shuttle; a case containing three pairs of steel scissors, a slim round pincushion and a box for packets of needles.

Collection of wooden pieces decorated with Fern or Seaweed design. Top left: a wool ball, decorated in brown with a lighter Fern design. It has a hole in the top of the lid through which to pull the end of the ball carried inside, and a cord loop for hanging over the wrist. Top right: an octagonal cotton box; it has eight pegs, two for each of four different thicknesses of cotton, space for a thimble and holes for needles. This is an unusual type. It is decorated with Fern design in reds and greens and has a Clarks 'Anchor' label inside the lid. Bottom from left: small double-ended roll pincushion covered in red fabric, and with the same decoration as the octagonal box; a small round pincushion decorated with Seaweed pattern, with a blue velvet pincushion; star-shaped Fern-decorated thread winder; a Fern-decorated container (the top removed), for tambour hooks and handle. These are missing.

Four examples of beautiful coloured prints under glass, with mirrors on the reverse side. Two needlecases and two pincushions.

A group showing beadwork. Top left: an unusual Mauchline beadworking box. The top lifts off revealing space inside for spare beads. The small cavity in the top is velvet-covered and holds beads in use, for ease of working. Bottom: a packet of extra long needles; a cylindrical needle-case decorated with blue and yellow beads; a beaded pincushion in two colours; a flat needlecase (the top removed). Top right: several bundles of beads as they were sold.

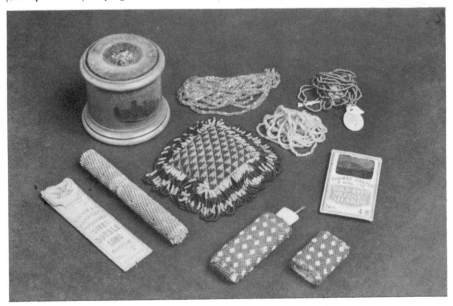

A display of various needlecrafts and related work. The corner of the tablecloth, held in an embroidery frame, is embroidered in cut-out white work. Moving clockwise and starting at the bottom centre of the circle: ribbons and an old packet of needles; a needlecase decorated in flowers in ribbon embroidery; an ivory and wood tool for 'French knitting'; a needlecase embroidered in the style of a sampler, with the alphabet, numbers, and 'Cury School 1848'; a pincushion and two needlecases embroidered on punched cards, the pincushion edged with mauve silk ribbon and the needlecases in dark blue and pink; two unused cards; a small group of Dorset buttons, made by sewing buttonhole stitch over a bone ring, and then weaving in an additional design; a small chatelaine in crochet, the items suspended on pink silk ribbon; to the right, two tatting shuttles, one in ivory, and one in tortoiseshell, with an example of the work; two packets of Flora Macdonald needles.

NEEDLEWORK AND RELATED ACTIVITIES

The term 'needlework' covers a wide field of sewing and embroidery, but there are other related activities using the hands and it may be helpful to the collector of the accessories used in them to describe briefly some of the main types.

Embroidery is perhaps the best known. This is the use of a needle to stitch various designs and patterns in white or coloured threads on linen or other materials. Frequently an embroidery frame will be used to keep the work flat and evenly stretched. Other types of embroidery are carried out on holed canvas. In the past a popular form of counted thread work was the sampler; some of the most charming of these were made by little children as an exercise in various stitches.

Beadwork was a popular activity in Regency and Victorian days. Tiny beads were threaded with an extremely fine needle on to a thread and then used to decorate all kinds of useful articles.

Several crafts involved knots used in

9

a variety of ways. Tatting, perhaps the best known of these today and still popular, involved the use of an elliptically shaped shuttle on to which the thread was wound. This thread produced knots on a separate thread held by the other hand. Knotting shuttles are a larger type of the same shape. Netting and macrame (the latter is enjoying a revival today) also involved making knots, though only netting required special tools, with the necessary netting needle and gauges, as still used by fishermen, and a netting clamp with a hook for commencing the work.

Cordmaking was a useful art, carried out with the lucet, a now scarce and expensive tool.

When making clothing and bed linen, many long seams had to be sewn, and a valuable aid for this purpose was the pincushion clamp or hemming bird, to which the material could be pinned while the clamp was attached to the table to keep the material taut.

Tambouring was carried out with a special hook attached to a handle. The material was stretched on an embroidery frame and the fine hook inserted from the top caught the thread held underneath by the other hand, drawing it through in a series of chain stitches to outline a design.

THIMBLES AND THIMBLE CASES

Thimbles have a long history and were made as a result of the need to protect the fingers when pushing a needle which was not polished into tough materials. Since smooth, shiny needles have been manufactured and lighter fabrics used, usually only gentle pressure from the fingertip has been required, so it has been possible to make thimbles from lighter, less durable materials, and many have been elaborately decorated. Among the collector's items are many, such as those of porcelain, glass and wood, which are more decorative than practical, although porcelain examples used to be regarded as useful in that they did not catch delicate materials.

Old porcelain thimbles have now become extremely scarce and expensive, and those most likely to be found will be fairly modern hand-painted items. Very attractive signed and hand-painted thimbles are currently being made by Royal Worcester, and others at the Caverswall Pottery. Numerous other transfer-printed models are freely available and appear in some personal collections.

Silver thimbles are the most likely collector's items to be found today and exist in a large variety of styles and decoration. Some have a semi-precious stone in the top or have designs and messages engraved round the lower edge.

They were made as commemorative souvenirs, for example for a jubilee or coronation, and sometimes to advertise a product. Some silver thimbles are enamelled and these can be very attractive. Gold thimbles are also interesting to the collector and, though not always hall-marked, are desirable.

One of the most serviceable thimbles was that which appeared under the trade name of Dorcas. It was made from a layer of steel sandwiched between two layers of silver, this type of construction making it particularly durable.

Other thimbles encountered include various designs in brass and advertising thimbles made in aluminium, sometimes with a coloured glass top, and bearing the name of a product on a coloured band round the lower edge.

Occasionally, rarer items are found, such as those made of ivory, vegetable ivory and mother-of-pearl (sometimes with a gilt band); these mainly originated from France. Another rare type is tortoiseshell decorated with gold or silver inlay or pique. Finally there are the fairly common examples made in early plastics

Tailor's thimbles have a hole in the top, as tailors customarily used the side of the thimble.

Hunt the Thimble used to be a pop-

10

A collection of thimbles. Left to right, top to bottom: modern hand-painted, signed porcelain, by Caverswall; modern porcelain decorated in dark blue and gold enamel, a copy of a Georgian design; modern Worcester porcelain hand-painted and signed flower design; modern turned wood; modern Spode porcelain, decorated in turquoise and gold; Worcester porcelain, hand-painted signed picture of birds. Second row: French silver with amethyst top; silver with steel top; silver finger guard; English hallmarked silver design; mother-of-pearl with gilt band and base. Third row: turned rosewood; four silver examples; wood with deep red stone in the top. Fourth row: brass decorated with Greek key pattern on the base; aluminium advertising 'Nugget Boot Polish'; metal with thread cutter on the side; aluminium 'Bonnie Scotland'; brass tailor's thimble.

Collection of thimble holders. Clockwise from bottom left: a brass chatelaine bucket with thimble; green velvet slipper with tassel; rectangular brass container with chain; blue velvet jockey cap (the top removed); plastic thimble-shaped container; purple velvet shoe; egg-shaped brass container with chain (open).

ular childish game, and one can speculate that a mother, having mislaid her precious and indispensable sewing aid, enlisted the aid of her children to find it, and thus was born the game.

Thimble cases are practical in more ways than one, and there is seemingly no end to the variety and ingenuity displayed in making these highly collectable items. They appear in all the souvenir wares, carved and turned wood, including bog-oak, ivory and vegetable ivory, tortoiseshell and mother-of-pearl. These last are often egg-shaped or in the shape of a miniature knife box and, though desirable, are now very scarce.

Acorn or beehive-shaped examples, the top unscrewing to reveal the space for a thimble, are fairly common, and wood and vegetable ivory appear as an egg in an egg-cup.

Leather cases in the shape of a thimble are found, and also some very attractive beadwork decorated items. Another charming variety is the small shoe, in velvet or glass, containing the thimble.

Thimble cases also sometimes incorporate some other essential tool, for example a needlecase, or a thimble and finger guard nestle closely together in the same case. The finger guard was to protect the finger of the hand not using the needle, preventing the needle being stuck into the finger supporting the fabric.

Collection of wooden thimble holders. Top row: a turned rosewood urn-shape; a walnut, with viewer in the stalk; an ivory-decorated ebony egg-cup, with a vegetable ivory egg (removed). Middle row: a vegetable ivory acorn; a wooden acorn; a turned acorn on a stand. Bottom row: a red-dyed ivory barrel; another acorn; a bog-oak top hat with carved clover-leaf design.

A collection of combination pieces. Clockwise from left: a turret-shaped tapemeasure with a pin poppet in the base; a Mauchline egg-shaped sewing compendium, with thimble, tiny cotton reel and needleholder inside; a turned rosewood pincushion and waxer; an ivory and beaded thimble holder and needlecase; a Mauchline beehive-shaped sewing compendium; a Mauchline thimble holder and pincushion; an ivory and vegetable ivory tapemeasure and needlecase (the top removed), with tiny views of Torquay in the tapemeasure winding handle.

A collection of wooden needlecases. Clockwise from top left: a walnut box (the top removed), to hold packets of needles; a turned mahogany holder with a metal size indicator for sewing-machine needles on the top; a carved continental container in two colours, probably Austrian, and a similar one representing corn on the cob; an ivory umbrella with a tiny viewer in the handle, showing pictures of Ambleside; a turned wood example and two pea-pod shapes, one in ivory and one in wood.

13

A collection of needlecases. Clockwise from top left: an ebony horn-shape with a viewer in the knob, showing pictures of Rigi — a red silk ribbon winds out to hold the needles; a rectangular metal holder with a lever on the bottom of the side to push up the selected size; a cylindrical metal case with an arrow on the side to select the size of needle, which can then be shaken out through a hole in the top; turned vegetable ivory type; metal, similar to the upright item, with the words 'Cross Fox'; milk glass and brass cylinder with a tiny lid; silk and tassel-decorated tubular shape; ornately decorated brass cylinder.

NEEDLECASES

In the early days of needlework needles were scarce and expensive and because they were so small and easily mislaid a variety of containers was devised to contain them. Some were made in precious metals, but these are seldom found now. China and glass examples are fairly rare but do occasionally turn up. Most commonly they were in cylindrical shapes.

The more usual form is that of a needlebook: leaves of flannel, folded between two covers of harder material, and tied at the front with silk ribbon. These were made in all the souvenir wares, mother-of-pearl, carved or decorated ivory, painted wood, paper and embroidered card.

Another fairly common type is an umbrella shape in wood, ivory or bone.

Sometimes these have a tiny viewer, with magnified photographs of a popular resort, in the handle.

There is a great variety of wooden needlecases: turned and carved in many shapes and designs, such as animals; or continental ones, often in two coloured woods, and perhaps carved to resemble an ear of corn. There are many plain cylindrical shapes, others like a rolling pin, and yet another upright variety with a marked metal top, indicating compartments for different-sized needles.

The more specially sought-after varieties include wood or ivory items shaped like a pea pod, beadwork, and the very interesting Avery needlecases. These were made mostly in brass (although an early plastic item— a cradle—has been seen), by the Redditch needle-making firm of Avery. They come in a fascinating variety of ingenious shapes: for example barrows, fans, shells, a picture on an easel or a walnut on a leaf. The metal container held packets of needles. The name of Avery is always stamped on and some are marked with the Victorian registration mark, which enables them to be accurately dated. These cases are now rather scarce and have become expensive as they are much sought after.

Another type made by Avery and other manufacturers is a slim rectangular box with a hinged top. Near the bottom is a small lever which can be moved to a number representing a size of needle. With the lid open, this movement pushes

A collection of paper, card and other needlecases. Top row: a folding paper casket (separately illustrated open), with a picture of King Edward VII on the top, the words 'Forget-me-not' and the Union Jack and French flag on the side; a black-painted needlebook with a flower design and a verse. Middle row: a velvet-covered card box, decorated with a Victorian scrap and a love message; green silk-covered bead-decorated bellows, lined with pale pink; a cardboard box decorated with a needleprint; an imitation ivory needlebook, 'A present from Bowness'. Bottom row: a Mauchline needlebook with transfer prints of Torquay on either side; a folding-leaved punched card example decorated with sentimental scraps; a decorated ivory needlebook.

up a metal container with a needle of that size.

Brass and other metals were used for embossed cylindrical containers, some of which are larger to hold bodkins for threading ribbon or elastic; and there are some elaborately decorated articles in book form.

Paper and card needlebooks and boxes are among the more charming collector s items, though because of their fragile nature not many have survived. There are paper caskets of many shapes; needlebooks made from embroidered, punched cards, this being a popular craft in Victorian times; and little boxes the size of a packet of needles, decorated on top with one of the attractive prints made by George Baxter or one of his licensees. These prints were made in sheets of the required size and came to be known as needleprints. Perhaps the most charming paper caskets are those made to look like a box, the top and sides decorated with coloured pictures. When the lid is lifted the sides fall separately, to reveal a delightful silk-lined interior, each of the sides holding a packet of needles under a ribbon, and in the centre a much smaller square box with a removable lid and containing a thimble.

ABOVE: Folding paper needlecase with the inside shown. The lining is pale pink silk. There is a packet of needles under each ribbon and a thimble in the central small box.

BELOW: Collection of pincushions. Clockwise from left: turned walnut wood with a rose-pink cushion; carved and pierced ivory with a red cushion on a carved coquilla nut base; green cushion on a carved and pierced ivory stand; a dainty turned rosewood stand with a rose-pink cushion; a plain turned wood container with a pale blue silk cushion. Centre: miniature early Tunbridge bowl with a pink cushion.

A collection of pincushions. Clockwise from left: a tiny square patchwork type with tiny pins inserted in a regular pattern; standing on its side, one in dark red leather with a gold design; an octagonal shell-decorated example, with a picture of the Crystal Palace on the reverse side; a circular pin wheel with a hand-painted coastal scene, finished with a silk ribbon; a playing card, in white silk with red-painted diamonds, the pins inserted round the outside; brown circular silk cushion, the divisions marked in gold and finished with brown and gold ribbon. Centre: plain gilded wood with purple velvet.

PINCUSHIONS AND EMERY CUSHIONS

Pincushions and emery cushions introduce us to the wealth of skill and ingenuity exercised by Victorian and Edwardian needlewomen. It would be impossible to catalogue them all, for one is always coming across something new. How often one longs to know whose fingers sewed the tiny stitches which made the minute patchwork pincushions or threaded the tiny beads with extremely fine needles to form the intricate designs. Scraps of left-over fabric, stuffed with bran or sheep's wool to prevent the pins from rusting, were fashioned into ever more imaginative shapes, such as flowers, stars, baskets and shoes.

Miniature jockey caps also turn up occasionally.

The talented amateur artists of the period had scope to demonstrate their skill in pin wheels, with a picture painted on silk or fine fabric. The wheel was made from two fabric-covered circles of card joined together, the pins being stuck round the outside between the layers. Knitting and crochet were also used to cover small pin balls which could be suspended from the waist.

Manufacturers produced pincushions in all the usual souvenir wares, often round but also shaped like hearts, diamonds and clubs. Ivory and mother-of

A collection of metal pincushions. Clockwise from left: a small black pug dog with a red velvet cushion; a bird with a blue velvet back; a shoe, with a picture of the Woolworth building in New York on the tongue; a donkey; a brass pig with a green cushion; a small brass box with a loose lid and a green cushion.

pearl were popular, two flat circles or other shapes enclosing a narrow pincushion. More unusual were tiny ivory bellows or barrows.

Natural shells of many types were pressed into use for pincushions and make an attractive addition to a collection, as do those in the form of china animals or pieces of fruit.

Wood or metal are used in many ways, the former making a turned stand topped by a velvet pincushion, or a carved bog-oak kitchen utensil, such as a cauldron or saucepan. Birds and animals in base metal are found in variety, together with the much sought-after brass pigs.

Silver pincushions are in the luxury class and are now scarce and expensive. English hallmarked items, mostly dating from the early twentieth century, are usually animals or birds, but fish, shoes or even a tiny cradle may be found. Continental silver items, such as baskets, are delightful and delicately made.

Another now scarce item, but one well worth searching for, is a pin poppet These mostly date from the late eight-

eenth century and appear in a variety of shapes, perhaps a pear or an acorn, while a pine cone is illustrated. The top unscrews to reveal a tiny silk pincushion, to hold much smaller pins than those now generally in use.

Two larger types of pincushion may also interest the collector: the layette, and those given by sailors and soldiers to their girl friends as love tokens. The former was a popular gift to the mother expecting a new baby and was usually made in pillow or flower shapes, with a design in flowers and a welcome message pricked out in large pins. The sailors' and soldiers' cushions were very elaborate, often heart-shaped, incorporating decorative glass-headed pins, woven silk messages and pictures, together with the name of the regiment.

Pincushion-topped boxes are fairly common. Many were lead-weighted and could be used to anchor material while sewing. Many of these date from Regency times, while some later boxes had lift-off or sliding lids which reveal a compartment for small sewing items or trinkets.

ABOVE LEFT: A layette pincushion. The pins make a design of hearts, flowers and leaves with the message 'Welcome as the Spring'.

ABOVE RIGHT: A soldiers' pincushion. This is heart-shaped, decorated with glass-topped pins stuck through beads, a coloured woven silk message, flags and the regimental name and badge. The colouring is mainly green.

Pincushion boxes. Top left: one in figured walnut; the loose padded drop-in lid has been recovered. Top right: a Regency-style weighted pincushion in wood, decorated with a thin inlay in a lighter colour. Bottom: two Mauchline boxes: left, with a blue velvet-covered sliding lid; right, a small box with drawer and pink velvet cushion on top.

Left: two pin poppets: a painted wood pine cone and a wooden acorn shape in two colours, the tops removed to show the cushions. Right: a carved wood workbox vinaigrette.

Top row: emery cushions: an unmarked silver heart-shape with a soft chamois cushion; a small sack marked 'To keep your needles bright'; workbox-type mother-of-pearl and ivory round shape with pink silk-covered emery cushion inside. Bottom row: five waxers: one ivory decorated in black; two carved mother-of-pearl; another with a turquoise in the centre and one in carved ivory.

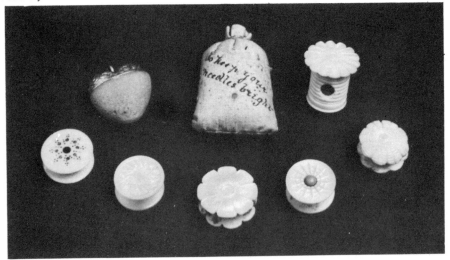

Another type of cushion, though not for pins, is the emery cushion. These come in many styles and materials, often as a matching piece in a fitted workbox. The cushion is filled with emery powder, which makes it feel heavier, and a needle was pushed in and out to remove rust. One type often met is a small fabric or knitted strawberry, decorated with small yellow beads to add realism.

TAPEMEASURES

The tapemeasure is a valuable aid to needlework and was often used by the lady of the house to check the measurement of materials which she bought from a travelling salesman calling at her door. Each household had a wooden yardstick from which to mark the measure in the days before tapemeasures were printed.

Early measures, up to about the middle of the nineteenth century, were marked in nails, a measurement of 2¼ inches; later the normal inch was used. There are many designs and tapemeasures could form a collection on their own. The earliest ones were wound into the container by a handle, the measure itself usually being made of silk ribbon. These were followed by the use of a spring mechanism.

As with other tools, tapemeasures were made in a great variety of materials and shapes. Wind-in examples come in silver, sometimes with a ring attached to hang on a chatelaine chain. Shells were used; metal appeared as animals, birds or household objects such as clocks and coffee grinders. Buildings, lamps, a coronation coach, a sewing machine and other novelties were popular. Ivory and vegetable ivory, mother-of-pearl and wood are also frequently used.

Spring mechanism examples come in great variety: china dolls or animals, metal novelties, advertising items, or a round shape with a picture in the top. Finally there are many in early plastic materials, such as baskets of fruit and flowers, ships, heads, dice, hats and pieces of fruit, etc.

A collection of tapemeasures. Top row: a bell shape in lignum vitae wood with an ivory handle; a realistically coloured wooden apple; one in turned wood; elaborately carved ivory, the top winding in the tape. Middle row: workbox matching type in mother-of-pearl and ivory, with a red silk tape; Tunbridge Stickware with green ribbon; mother-of-pearl. Bottom row: vegetable ivory, with 'A present from Ventnor', with a viewer in the ivory handle; ivory decorated in black; a small wooden type wound in by a handle on the top; one in turned rosewood.

21

A group of novelty tapemeasures. A brass watermill; the tape winds in by the wheel. A lamp decorated with a painted design; the tape winds in by the top and ends with the dragonfly on the side. A round brass type, decorated with a lithograph of a Georgian man; this has a spring mechanism. A miniature coffee grinder. A colour print of the Crystal Palace under glass, with a mirror on the back; this is also a spring mechanism. A hallmarked silver round shape, with a mother-of-pearl top and bottom.

A selection of thread holders. Top row: a reel holder with carved mother-of-pearl top; an early Tunbridge cotton barrel (the spindle is missing); a turned wood cotton barrel; an ebony multi-reel; a mother-of-pearl flower-shape reel holder. Bottom row: another in mother-of-pearl; a carved ivory cotton barrel; an ivory reel (the centre top removes to reveal a container for pins); an ivory cotton barrel of an early design; and another ivory reel complete with thread.

A collection of thread winders. Top row: two in mother-of-pearl, on either side of a leather-covered box, containing winders in different kinds of wood, each one labelled with the botanical and common names. Second row: a wooden star, two mother-of-pearl shapes and a wooden flower shape, decorated with poker work. Third row: one in ivory on either side of an unusual mother-of-pearl shape. Lower row: one in ivory and one in mother-of-pearl on either side of an amusing wooden bear.

THREAD HOLDERS, WINDERS, WAXERS AND REEL-STANDS

Many workboxes during the early part of the nineteenth century were fitted with cotton barrels to hold thread. The barrel had a spindle inside and a hole in the side out of which the thread could be drawn. They were made in ivory and wood including Tunbridge ware. The barrels were succeeded by reel holders, mostly with a carved mother-of-pearl top and bone base, joined by a slim hollow metal rod, one end fitting inside the other. Carved ivory reels were also made, but they are not very common. Wooden cotton reels did not make their appearance until 1820-1830.

A large variety of reel boxes were made in all the souvenir wares and plain polished wood. These boxes have pegs inside to hold the reels and holes in the sides, through which the thread can emerge; they often have a label inside the lid advertising Clarks 'Anchor' cotton. Some other manufacturers' labels are also found, but not very often.

In the past embroidery silks were very soft and 'catchy', so the skeins were wound on to thread winders to prevent the silk from becoming tangled. There are many different shapes made in a variety of materials, including mother-of-pearl, ivory, bone, wood (in the souvenir wares), plastic and even glass.

A mahogany reel box, probably Regency, the lid lined with green padded silk. The centre rod, holding the reels on brass wires, lifts out by small brass knobs. The lower drawer is secured with a wire which pushes down into the drawer, through the side of the box (the wire can just be seen on the right-hand side of the box).

Cotton boxes. Clockwise from left: rectangular in wood with a painted sliding top, revealing inside three reels of John Lewis thread of different thicknesses; a Mauchline box with a view of Tenby; a black-painted box with a verse and coloured flower decoration; a vase-shaped wooden container, decorated with flowers, with a tiny pincushion on top; a Mauchline milk-bucket shape with a print of Jedburgh Abbey (the pincushion top removes to reveal a reel).

The thread used for sewing was not originally mercerised and smooth, and so the cotton was drawn across a thread waxer to make it slide easily through the material and to strengthen it. Beeswax or candle wax was used and it was also possible to buy small cakes of wax wrapped in foil, which could then be fixed between two circles of carved mother-of-pearl, ivory, bone or wood. Waxers are quite often found combined with tapemeasures or pincushions.

In order to keep reels of cotton at hand and ready to use, reel-stands were used. They were made of metal or turned wood on a circular base with revolving or fixed galleries and had pegs on which to place the reels. The stand was usually topped with a pincushion, and some had a wooden acorn shape to hold a thimble. The earlier ones are small and dainty, while many of the later ones are heavy and more clumsy. Especially large ones were used in haberdashery shops.

Two early nineteenth-century reel stands. The left-hand one is topped with a brown velvet pincushion. The gallery holding the reels and thimble revolves. The smaller stand is made of rosewood and is only about 5 inches tall (125 mm).

SCISSORS

Scissors, an essential tool of the needle-woman, were made in a great variety of shapes, sizes and materials, including silver gilt, silver, steel and even ivory. Many have beautifully decorated handles, mother-of-pearl and tortoiseshell occasionally being used. Those made in the shape of a crane or stork are popular, and another interesting type of collector's item is a matching set in a case. One early form of scissors is made like a miniature pair of sheep shears. Folding scissors are fairly common, some simply folding so that the sharp part of the blades is not exposed, and others folding completely, revealing only the ivory or tortoiseshell handles. Scissors of a special type with a section cut out of the blade for cutting buttonholes are fairly common, but occasionally rarer types turn up, such as a long-bladed pair, with inches and measurements marked on the blade.

Another useful related tool is a seam-knife, or seam ripper. This has a flat, pointed blade, sharp on both sides, for speedy unpicking of seams.

A collection of scissors. From top to bottom: a large decorative steel pair; an ornately decorated, hallmarked silver-handled pair with steel blades, and a pair in stork or crane design; a pair in silver gilt in matching sheath (the handles are decorated with crowns and the words 'Honi soit qui mal y pense'), and a dainty pair also with silver-gilt handles; two plainer pairs of steel; two wafer lifters with ivory handles; a pair of buttonhole scissors, and a pair in ivory; a pair of tortoiseshell-handled folding scissors, and two minute pairs, those on the right-hand side no more than an inch (25 mm) long.

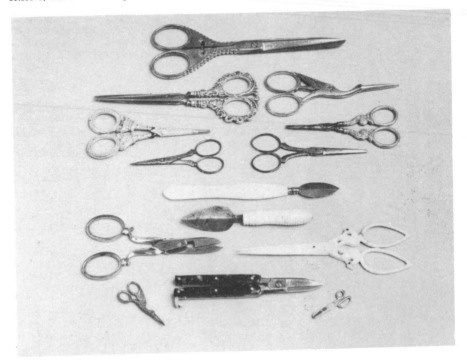

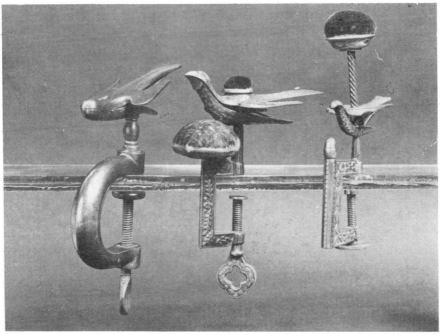

Three hemming birds. From left to right: a heavy bronze early type; a bird in lighter-weight bronze, with two pincushions, and the patent date stamped on the edge of one wing; a brass bird with a blue velvet pincushion on top of the spiral-shaped rod. The acorn on the clamp unscrews to reveal a holder for needles.

MISCELLANEOUS ACCESSORIES

Sewing clamps, or *hemming birds*, are much sought after and have become extremely rare and expensive. They are made mainly in brass or bronze. A metal clamp to fix to the table is topped by a bird whose beak opens when the tail is depressed. The closed beak then holds the material firm while sewing proceeds. One or two pincushions are usually incorporated, and sometimes a container for needles.

Winding clamps, usually made in ivory, bone or wood, were supplied in pairs. The clamps had revolving cages on top, over which the skein of thread was placed to be wound into a ball (which could be placed in the cup-shaped piece on top of the cage, if necessary) or on to a thread winder.

Pincushion clamps were simply a pincushion on top of a clamp and were used, in a similar way to hemming birds, to anchor the material with pins.

Netting clamps had a hook attached to a clamp and were used to commence netting.

Sometimes several of these will be found in combination, and tapemeasures, too, may be included.

Tambour hook and spool knave. The tambour hook was usually made of ivory or mother-of-pearl, and the ivory handle concealed a metal hook, which by means of a screw could be fitted into position for working. The spool-knave was used in conjunction with this tool; it consists of a ring to slip over the wrist, and from this is suspended a removable, re-

Three wooden clamps. Left: a rosewood tapemeasure topped with a pincushion. Centre: an early Tunbridge pincushion and tapemeasure clamp; the tapemeasure is the original silk ribbon. The wording on the small label on the front is 'Give me the love that lasts'. Right: a rosewood winding clamp with a revolving cage. This would have been one of a pair.

A collection of tatting shuttles. Top: a simple wooden type. Second row: a slim carved ivory one and a plain ivory one on either side of a hook with a chain and ring to slip on the finger. Third row: two tortoiseshell examples. Bottom: a fine filigree silver type.

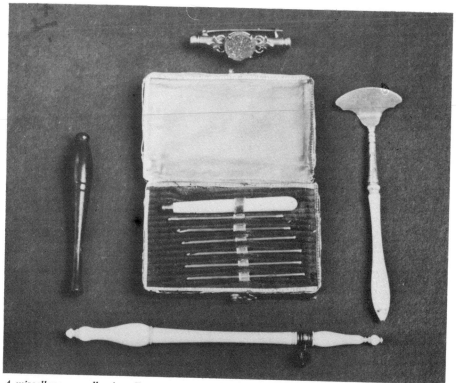

A miscellaneous collection. Top: a nanny or sewing brooch. Centre: a styptic pencil in rosewood holder (these are quite frequently found in workboxes); a case made of cardboard and lined in pale and rose-pink silk, containing a crochet set of a handle and six different-sized hooks; a seam presser, with ivory handle. Bottom: a fine ivory tambour hook complete with one hook inside the handle.

volving rod between two metal stays; the ball or reel of thread is inserted on to the metal rod, and thus runs freely while work is in progress.

Tatting and knotting shuttles. The shuttles are larger and smaller sizes of the same shape and can be very decorative. Most of those found today are in carved ivory, plain ivory, bone, mother-of-pearl, tortoiseshell, and also metal and plastics. Some of the metal examples have a hook attached. This is necessary for the work, but usually a separate tool is preferred. A chain with a small hook attached, joined to a ring to slip on the finger, is sometimes found.

Hand coolers. These are egg-shaped pieces of stone and were used to keep the hands fresh when handling fine fabrics.

Workbox vinaigrettes and powder sprinklers. The vinaigrette is a small box, usually in wood or ivory. The top unscrews to reveal a small perforated lid to an inner container, in which could be placed lavender flowers or wadding soaked in aromatic vinegars. Powder sprinklers were used to keep the hands dry and fresh while working.

Sewing or nanny brooch. These come strictly under the heading of jewellery but are of interest to the collector of needlework tools; they date from Edwardian times. The brooch has a thicker than usual bar, often with a round or diamond-shaped goldstone set in the

29

centre. One end of the bar unscrews, to reveal a hollow metal tube, containing needle and pins, with black and white cotton wound round the tube. Children's nurses wore the brooch, probably at the high neck of the blouse, and should one of their small charges tear a garment or lose a button, an immediate repair could be carried out.

Netting needles and gauges. These were usually made in wood or bone. The needle is a flat tool, with an open forked shape at one or both ends. The gauges are flat pieces of different widths used to fix the size of the holes in the netting.

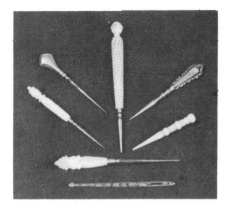

A collection of stilettos with a bodkin at the bottom in engraved silver. Above this is a stiletto in steel with mother-of-pearl handle. Others anticlockwise: ivory; steel with a silver handle; brass with a carved ivory handle; another with a silver handle and one with a turned ivory handle.

Two lucets for cardmaking. Left: imitation tortoiseshell. Right: wood.

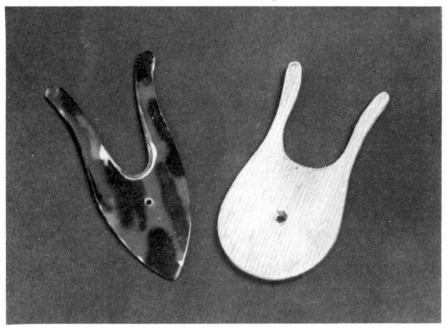

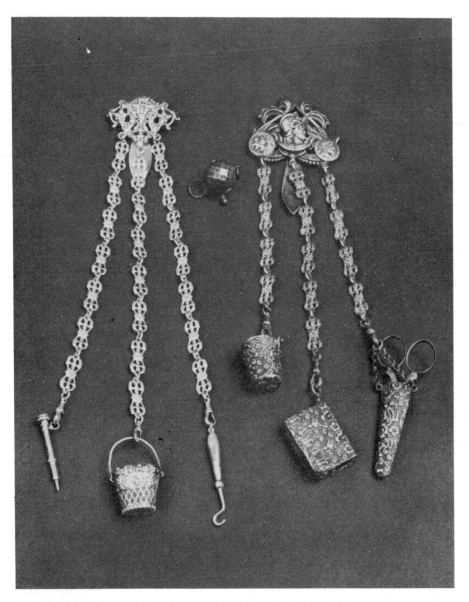

Two chatelaines. On the left, a silver example, hallmarked 1897. The chains end in swivel clips, with a pencil, a buttonhook with a blue lace agate in the handle, and a continental silver basket pincushion. The pencil and buttonhook are both hallmarked silver of a contemporary date. In the centre is an early nineteenth-century round steel chatelaine tapemeasure. On the right is a brass chatelaine, with three matching items attached by swivel clips, including a brass thimble in a bucket.

FURTHER READING

Andere, Mary. *Old Needlework Boxes and Tools.* David & Charles, 1971.
Colby, Averil. *Pincushions.* Batsford, 1975.
Groves, Sylvia. *The History of Needlework Tools and Accessories.* David & Charles, 1973.
Holmes, Edwin. *Thimbles.* Gill and McMillan, Dublin, 1976.
Pinto, E. and Eva. *Tunbridge and Scottish Souvenir Woodware.* Bell, 1969.
Pinto, E. H. *Treen and Other Wooden Bygones.* Bell, 1969.
Rogers, Gay Ann. *An Illustrated History of Needlework Tools.* John Murray, 1983.
Whiting, Gertrude. *Old Time Tools and Toys of Needlework.* Dover Publications, 1971.

PLACES TO VISIT

Bethnal Green Museum of Childhood, Cambridge Heath Road, London E2 9PA. Telephone: 01-980 2415. Fine collection of workboxes and caskets.
Birmingham Museum and Art Gallery, Chamberlain Square, Birmingham B3 3DH. Telephone: 021-235 2834. The Pinto Collection of wooden bygones.
Cambridge and County Folk Museum, 2/3 Castle Street, Cambridge CB3 0AQ. Telephone: Cambridge (0223) 355159.
Gawthorpe Hall, Padiham, near Burnley, Lancashire BB12 8UA. Telephone: Burnley (0282) 78511.
Guildford Museum, Castle Arch, Quarry Street, Guildford, Surrey GU1 3SX. Telephone: Guildford (0483) 503497 extension 3540.
Old House Museum, Cunningham Place, Bakewell, Derbyshire.
Portsmouth City Museum and Art Gallery, Museum Road, Old Portsmouth, Hampshire PO1 2LJ. Telephone: Portsmouth (0705) 827261.
Shaftesbury Local History Museum, Gold Hill, Shaftesbury, Dorset. Telephone: Shaftesbury (0747) 2157 or 3426.
Tudor House Museum, Bugle Street, Southampton, Hampshire. Telephone: Southampton (0703) 224216 or 223855 extension 2768. Large collection of needlework tools.
There are small collections of needlework tools in many museums and National Trust houses.

ACKNOWLEDGEMENTS

The author gratefully acknowledges the loan of thimbles and thimble cases by Mrs D. Sainsbury. All the photographs were taken by Mr J. Watson of Frederick Watson & Son Ltd, Bridport, Dorset.